Cover Photograph: Liverpool Pier Head, 1911. Courtesy of Chevron
Photographic.   Hand colouring by George Baxendale.
Back Cover: Photograph by David Williams.

Typesetting: Typebase, Liverpool
Origination: Creation Graphics, Birkenhead
Printed by: Dah Hua Printing Press

ISBN 1 872568 03 3

Then and Now

The Changing Face of Liverpool

TEXT BY COLIN WILKINSON

PHOTOGRAPHS OF MODERN LIVERPOOL BY MICHAEL MEADOWS

The Bluecoat Press

Liverpool, Old and New, 1946

The people look posed but the message is clear, "out with the old, in with the new". Forty five years later, the flats are being pulled down and the old, Victorian terraces are being renovated.

Introduction

Liverpool is a mixture of buildings. Old and new, small and large ... all the result and evidence of three centuries of economic and social turmoil that saw a small, obscure fishing port grow into one of the most important commercial and trading centres in the world. The buildings that have survived are a reminder of the changes that have taken place.

Unlike York or Chester and many other cities, Liverpool does not have a history stretching back to pre-Roman times. Very little remains of its antiquarian past, although the medieval street pattern that once linked the castle to the river has survived as a distant reminder of the port's earliest years. In fact, the only two significant pre-nineteenth century buildings in the city centre are the Bluecoat Chambers (1716-18) and the Town Hall (1749, with substantial reconstruction in 1807). Liverpool is, therefore, a nineteenth and twentieth century city, a rich expression of architectural styles from the smart Georgian houses of Rodney Street and the neo-Classical masterpiece of St. George's Hall to the monumental dock warehouses of Jesse Hartley, the contrastingly thin, lineal beauty of Peter Ellis's Oriel Chambers and through to the twentieth century buildings that dominate the skyline; the Royal Liver Building, the Offices of the Mersey Docks and Harbour Company, the Anglican Cathedral and the Metropolitan Cathedral.

Visitors invariably express their amazement at the legacy of fine architecture that Liverpool has retained and, compared to many cities, a significant number of its key buildings have survived. However, changes have taken place that have had a major impact on the shape and look of the city. Although war damage was severe, it is the period of post-war reconstruction up to the mid 1970's that most radically changed the skyline. Comprehensive redevelopment to accommodate both the motor car and the projected demand for office space led to a wholesale destruction of key areas that irrevocably changed the character of the city. It is these changes that this book attempts to document, not in the negative sense of decrying all redevelopment, for without change Liverpool would still be an insignificant fishing port, but by drawing attention to buildings and streets that have been lost and the new developments that have replaced them. Whether the new is better than the old is for the reader to decide.

Acknowledgements

The photographs of modern Liverpool were taken by Michael Meadows. The photographs of old Liverpool came from a number of sources; in particular, Liverpool City Engineer's Department, Elsam, Mann and Cooper, Oxton Studios, Chevron Photographic and the Royal Commission for Historic Monuments of England. We would like to express our appreciation for their kind assistance.

Everton, 1925

It is difficult to imagine that, a century earlier, Everton was a small village on the outskirts of Liverpool. The population in 1831 was only 4518 but this rapidly grew to 109,812 by 1881. The mansions and villas were swept away and all traces of greenery disappeared. Today, the terraces have, in turn, been replaced and the area is reverting to attractive parkland.

The Changing Face of Liverpool

Once on a time this good old town was nothing but a village
Of fishermen and smugglers that ne'er attempted tillage;
But things are altered very much, such buildings and Naccapolis
It rivals far and soon will leave behind the Metropolis

Oh dear oh, for Liverpool's an altered town, oh dear oh.

Once on a time, were you inclined your weary limbs to lave, sir
In summer's scorching heat, in Mersey's cooling wave, sir,
You'd only just to go behind the old Church for the shore, sir
But now it's past Jack Langham's, half a mile or more, sir.

Oh dear oh, for Liverpool's an altered town, oh dear oh.

When things do change you scarce do know what next is sure to follow,
For mark the change in Derby Road that late was Plumpton's fellow;
Now Atkins found it out so smug and changed its etymology,
He clapped in it his wild beast show, now it's Garden of Zoology.

Oh dear oh, for Liverpool's an altered town, oh dear oh.

A market was on Shaw's Brown, and it remains there still, sir.
The Infirmary they have taken away and clapped on Brownlow Hill, sir.
There's Gloucester Street and Nelson Street have had an alteration,
They've pulled the most part of them down and built a railway station.

Oh dear oh, for Liverpool's an altered town, oh dear oh.

The spire of famed St.Thomas's that long had stood the weather,
Although it was so very high, they've downed it altogether;
And the Old Dock, the poor Old Dock, the theme of many a sonnet,
They've pulled it up and now have built a Custom House upon it.

Oh dear oh, for Liverpool's an altered town, oh dear oh.

In former times, if you had taken a walk through Queen's Square, sir,
You might have seen, if you had looked, a slashing rope
walk there, sir;
Yet all those things the public thought were getting very stale, sir,
On the rope walk they've a market and on the square a whale, sir.

'Liverpool's An Altered Town'. Street ballad c.1840.

An unsympathetic attitude towards change is not the prerogative of the present day, as the ballad illustrates. What today has in common with a century and a half ago is that fundamental upheavals to society bring into focus our anxieties for the future. Liverpool in the 1840's was undergoing a massive expansion in economic activity and physical size, fed by an astonishing growth in population. In the 1990's, the city is trying to adjust to an equally marked population decline in a period of what has been called post-industrial society. In both cases, the future could be looked upon as one of great opportunity.

The Victorians certainly took change in their stride as is indicated in Fraser's 'Guide to Liverpool' (1854):

"Never was there a town in Europe which sprang from such poverty and insignificance in so short a time. Streets and public edifices seem to have started into existence as the consequence of some mighty enchantment; hardly a vestige of the primitive fishing town remains, not a stone to stimulate antiquarian speculation. Every public building is modern; every locality has been charged by the spirit of improvement. The streets which were formerly so few in number, so mean in appearance, and but little used to the hum of business, are now countless, grand and forever busy ..."

Today, the opportunities for creating a better future are, ironically, driven partly by the decline in local population which has raised up the prospect of reducing housing densities, more sensitive landscaping and lifting the pressure on city centre space. There are many indications that these options are being taken up but, unlike the Victorians, there is a crisis in confidence about our cities that has made the public suspicious about change and redevelopment. The past (pre-War) has become a symbol of the 'golden era', before the Blitz and bulldozers did their worst to the city. This nostalgia for the past has been criticised for being misplaced; poverty, slum housing, unemployment and high mortality levels are not post-War inventions. Furthermore, too great an obsession with the past can create a reaction against the new, blocking positive ideas when change is essential to reverse decline. Nevertheless, changes to familiar surroundings are always unsettling and often the criticism of insensitive planning is hard to discount.

The post-war period, in particular, has borne the brunt of this criticism. Ironically, the Town and Country Planning Act of 1947 was intended to protect the erosion of our architectural heritage yet, it has been claimed, more damage has been wreaked on our cities in the forty odd years since then, than in over four hundred years up to the passing of the Act. Of course, one cannot blame a single piece of legislation for the attack on our townscapes but there has been a universal failure to protect what is good and worth preserving and an unwillingness to tackle such key problems as the motor car, changing demands for housing and the excesses of the speculative property developers.

The nineteenth century changed Liverpool dramatically, but the Victorians were, in general, building on new land and little of great significance was pulled down. Since 1945, however, the list of important buildings lost is depressing; the Custom House, the Sailors' Home, the Overhead Railway, the Goree Piazzas, the Theatre Royal, St John's Market, Queen Square, Duke's Dock and Benn's Gardens represent a sad starting point. In retrospect, none of these should have ben pulled down. The Custom House and Goree Piazzas were firebombed during the War but both were structurally sound and could have been renovated. The Overhead Railway was lost because the cost of repair was considered too high at the time. St John's Market, the Theatre Royal and Queen Square all fell foul of the unbelievably bad civic centre scheme that was mercifully stopped in its tracks but not before a whole network of busy streets and squares was lost forever. Benn's Gardens, a tiny enclave of early merchants' houses, made way for undistinguished new Law Courts; Duke's Dock, one of the port's earliest warehouses, was pulled down to make way for a short-lived transit shed. Most astonishingly, the Sailors' Home survived until 1974 before being pulled down to be replaced by ... an advertising hoarding!

Needless destruction enrages everyone who cares about their city. Once a building has been destroyed it can never be replaced. William Morris, in founding the National Society for the Protection of Ancient Buildings in 1877, put his case succinctly;

"It has been truly said that these old buildings do not belong to us only; that they belonged to our forefathers and they will belong to our descendants unless we play them false. They are not in any sense our property, to do as we like with them, we are only trustees for those who come after us ..."

The twentieth century has not been unsympathetic to Liverpool. Many of its greatest buildings have been built since 1900. Work on the Anglican Cathedral commenced in 1903, although it was a criminal act to pull down St Peter's Church, in Church Street, as a direct consequence. Tower Buildings (1906) is in no way inferior to the building it replaced. The Crown and Vines public houses on Lime Street are fine examples of Edwardian Baroque and neighbouring Adelphi Hotel is one of Liverpool's grandest buildings.

Above all, the Pier Head group dominates the city and give it a visual identity that few other cities possess. The magnificent Royal Liver Building (completed in 1911) is one of the great, romantic buildings of this century. Built on reclaimed dockland, it is a constant reminder that good architecture is the most public expression of its time and must always be encouraged.

In fact, Liverpool has been fortunate in attracting architects of the highest calibre. Perhaps the greatest, yet least appreciated, was Herbert J. Rowse, architect of India Buildings, the Mersey Tunnel, Martin's Bank Headquarters, the Philharmonic Hall and George's Dock Build-

ings. The legacy of Rowse is astonishing yet his name is rarely mentioned except in books on city architecture. He deserves better!

Sadly, post-war architecture has only one great name to conjure with; Sir Frederick Gibberd, whose modernistic Metropolitan Cathedral has been affectionately embraced by the people of Liverpool. Had the original Lutyen's cathedral been built, Liverpool would have possessed one of the greatest buildings of our time but it was not to be and Gibberd's building has taken its welcome place on the city's skyline.

Good architecture is essential, although it is often better left to future generations to decide what 'good' represents. Georgian architecture only really became fashionable after the formation of the Georgian Group in 1937. Similarly, the reaction against Victorian architecture reached its height in the 1950's, culminating in the disgraceful demolition of Euston Arch in 1962. The public and press reaction against such official vandalism provoked a reappraisal of the Victorian legacy, although many fine buildings were to disappear over the next decade. Fashions do change but must we continually make the same mistake of pulling down good buildings because they do not fit in with current whims?

Looking at the photographs of Liverpool today, it is encouraging to see many significant improvements to the city centre. Pedestrianisation has given us the opportunity to enjoy looking at the wealth of fine buildings; the cleaning of facades has revealed ornamentation and stonework as it was originally meant to be seen. The refurbishment of St John's Precinct is an improvement on the brutal, concrete exterior which seemed to summarise all that was wrong with modern architecture. Above all, it is the sympathetic conservation of such key buildings as the Albert Dock, Wapping Warehouse and the Lyceum Club that give hope for the future, for here we have an understanding that conservation, although costly, is financially astute. The effect of saving the Lyceum and converting it to an appropriate use has transformed the future of Bold Street. Once the 'Bond Street of the North' but for twenty years in decline, Bold Street now has the chance to re-establish itself as a distinguished shopping thoroughfare.

This spirit of change is giving the city centre a fighting chance. Queen Square, once a centre for dozens of small businesses, is top of a list of priority areas along with the Duke Street area and London Road. In each case, there is a pledge to preserve the existing important architecture and to incorporate it within the new plans. After years of uncertainty, there is good reason to be optimistic about the future. What has been lost cannot be replaced and there are still threats to important sites, particularly in the suburbs; but the prevailing opinion is to make the most of the city's heritage and to promote it as British 'City of Architecture'. Liverpool deserves nothing less!

Sailors' Home, 1880

What possible benefit was gained by pulling down the Sailors' Home? John Cunningham's lodging house for seaman was based on an Elizabethan mansion on the outside and, internally, possessed a fascinating courtyard with tiers of cast-iron balconies. Little attempt was made to find an alternative use for it when it became vacant. Instead, it was shamelessly demolished, in 1974. Had it survived, it would have unquestionably have been awarded Grade One building status, yet another important feather in Liverpool's cap. As it is, all we are left with is a hole in the ground to show for this act of municipal vandalism.

Liverpool Landing Stage, 1912

In 1874, the 2000 foot Floating Landing Stage was about to open to the public when it was almost destroyed by fire. Rebuilt, it finally opened in 1876. Added to over the years until it was nearly half a mile long, the Landing Stage was the largest floating structure in the world. The terminal for great ocean liners as well as ferries, it was the final point of departure for millions of emigrants.

Liverpool Landing Stage

The wooden stage has recently been replaced with a shorter but more permanent concrete structure. Sadly, liners no longer dominate the waterfront but the ferries continue to ply their trade to Wallasey and Birkenhead and back.

Pier Head Parade, 1902

George's Parade was constructed in 1771, the year Captain Cook circumnavigated the world. The parade was the entrance to the Landing Stage and was a favourite promenade and meeting place.

Pier Head Parade

In 1967, Pier Head was redeveloped. One advantage of the new building was the overhead promenade, which gave excellent views of the river. Architecturally, however, the scheme detracts from the grandeur of its setting and is now being replaced by a (hopefully) more sympathetic development.

George's Dock, 1907

A fascinating photograph showing the filling in of George's Dock prior to the building of the Royal Liver Building. The Head Offices of the Mersey Docks and Harbour Board had just opened for business, after some controversy amongst board members as to the cost incurred. A major bone of contention was the striking copper dome. "It seems to me that it is not part of the duty of the Board to beautify the town", complained one director. Happily, his argument did not win the day.

Royal Liver Building

The Royal Liver Friendly Society Building, to give its original title, was completed in 1911 to the design of Walter A. Thomas. The first large-scale reinforced concrete building in the world, it has become the unforgettable symbol of the city. Next to it, the Cunard Building (completed in 1916) is a more restrained but equally fine building. Beyond, the white tower of George's Dock Building hides the main ventilation shaft for the Mersey Tunnel.

The Church of Our Lady and St Nicholas, 1919

St Nicholas' Church represents continuity with Liverpool's medieval past, although little remains of the original church. In 1810, its spire collapsed, killing twenty two girls from a charity school in Moorfields. The church fronted George's Basin, until the turn of the century, and was surrounded by imposing warehouses and offices.'

The Church of Our Lady and St Nicholas
The Atlantic Tower Hotel is an interesting addition to the skyline. Equally dominant but somewhat less elegant are the offices of Royal Insurance. The Floating Roadway, in the foreground, was once the main access for traffic to the Landing Stage but is now fenced off.

Liverpool Overhead Railway, 1919

Perhaps the most poignant of all scenes. Why was the Overhead Railway demolished? Built in 1893, it was the first elevated railway in Europe. Running between Seaforth and Dingle, it offered passengers unrivalled views of the river and docks.

Strand Street

The Overhead Railway finally closed in 1956, to the disbelief of the Liverpool public. The Goree Warehouses disappeared two years later, giving the planners the opportunity to introduce a more effective road network. The result is a barren stretch of land that separates the city centre from the river and has none of the romance and excitement of the old street.

The Goree Piazzas, 1913

The Goree Piazzas were two massive warehouses, rebuilt in 1802 after a fire had destroyed earlier buildings. An impressive arcade ran the length of the warehouses. Washington Irving, the author of Rip Van Winkle, managed his brother's business from the Goree, named after an island, off Cape Verde, which was used as an entrepot during slaving days.

The Strand

It is hard to imagine that this stretch of roadway once comfortably fitted in the Overhead Railway and the Goree Piazzas with roads on either side. Once again, the motor car has triumphed and the city's heritage has been thrown away for short-term gain.

George's Dock, c.1885

George's Dock opened in 1771 and was Liverpool's third dock. The Goree warehouses ran along its side.

Goree

The small section of north bound carriageway has kept the name of the old warehouses but only St Nicholas' Church survives as a reminder of the nineteenth century. The dock was filled in to create the foundations for the Dock Office (and, later, the Royal Liver Building and Cunard Building).

Tower Buildings, 1906

Tower Buildings was an imposing, if somewhat undistinguished, Victorian building erected on the site of the medieval tower, which was demolished in 1819.

Tower Buildings

The present Tower Buildings was designed by W. Aubrey Thomas, architect of the Royal Liver Buildings. An early example of steel framed construction, it was completed in 1906. The facade was glazed in an experimental attempt to combat the city's soot and grime.

The Custom House, c.1880

What a magnificent compliment the Custom House would have made to the restored Albert Dock! Designed by John Foster junior and built on the site of the Old Dock, the Custom House consisted of two enormous wings with the centre surmounted by a large dome and cupola. Built with white freestone, the building opened in 1828 and housed the custom and excise offices and the main post office.

Canning Dock and Canning Place

The Pump House, on the right, shows what can be saved and put to new use. Sadly, such thinking came too late to stop the demolition of the Custom House. Although it suffered serious bomb damage during the Blitz, it was not beyond renovation. However, the City Fathers had other ideas, which included the deteriorating, totally unsympathetic steel and glass construction that now jars the eye.

Exchange Buildings, 1906

The first Exchange Buildings were erected in 1803 and were widely admired for their classical beauty. The Victorians demonstrated that civic vandalism is not the prerogative of any one age by replacing the buildings with an elaborate yet impressive Gothic structure. The Nelson Memorial, Liverpool's first public sculpture, remained as a centre piece in the quadrangle.

Exchange Buildings

The march of progress saw off the second building in the 1930's. The present building is a very ordinary example of inter-war architecture, totally out of scale with its setting. A refurbishment programme is underway, although a completely new development would be a far better solution.

The Cotton Exchange, Old Hall Street, 1906

The Cotton Exchange was built at the height of Liverpool's commercial success. The flamboyant exterior (by Matear and Simon) reflects the confidence of the booming cotton trade and was a fine example of Edwardian craftsmanship.

The Cotton Exchange

A building in name only, for the cotton trade which help create Liverpool's prosperity has long gone. The significance of such ties with the past was lost on the developers, who pulled down the facade and replaced it with a bland piece of modernism. Only the statue from the original building survives, dumped on the pavement in what seems an apologetic afterthought.

Old Haymarket, 1928

Old Haymarket, photographed from St John's Gardens, before work on the Mersey Tunnel commenced. Henry Tate bought his first grocery shop here before going on to found Tate and Lyle.

Mersey Tunnel Entrance

The Mersey Tunnel was one of the greatest engineering achievements of its time. Herbert J. Rowse's distinctive style is evident in every detail although the massive column that once dominated the entrance has unfortunately been removed.

Byrom Street, 1927

Byrom Street led out of Old Haymarket towards Scotland Road and was a bustling thoroughfare lined with shops and houses. The Technical School, on the right, is the last addition to the magnificent sweep of public buildings on William Brown Street.

Byrom Street

The Technical School still stands and looks better after stone-cleaning. Otherwise, the motor car rules. The concrete flyover won awards.

Springfield Mill, Walton Road 1919
The sad remains of one of Liverpool's last windmills gives poignant interest to its miserable setting.

Walton Road

The windmill has gone the way of all of Liverpool's other windmills, leaving a drab cul de sac brightened somewhat by the newly-decorated Springfield Hotel.

Scotland Road, 1908

Scotland Road was once one of the most lively streets in Liverpool. Notorious for its slums and poverty, it had a reputation for the generosity and fierce loyalty of its community.

Scotland Road

Sadly, Scotland Road fell victim to the internal combustion engine when the area was severed by new roads servicing the new Kingsway Tunnel. Already battered by the housing clearances of the 1950's and '60's, the community has been left fragmented, surrounded by forlorn patches of cleared land.

Browside, Everton, c.1880

Browside was famous for Molly Bushell's house, where Charles Dicken's favourite Everton toffee was first made in the 1760's (and from which Everton Football Club takes its nickname). In 1800, Everton was described as 'a pretty village with a view which embraces town, village, plain, pasture, river and ocean.' Thirty years later, a visitor reported that 'Everton now abounds with handsome walled pleasure grounds and well enclosed fields'.

Browside, Netherfield Road South.

Few areas can have seen so much change over two hundred years. From picturesque village to salubrious suburb; from salubrious suburb to densely packed slums; from slums to high rise flats and, finally, to impressive urban parkland.

Monument Place, London Road, 1897

The statue of George III presides over a prosperous London Road.

Monument Place, London Road

The statue still has pride of place and many of the buildings are still recognisable but London Road has suffered from a shift in population and changing shopping habits. Once busy shops are now empty, although new initiatives will, hopefully, reverse the area's decline.

Clayton Square, 1963

Clayton Square was originally laid out as an exclusive housing estate for the merchant classes. The merchants moved out and shops moved in to take advantage of the proximity of the square to the bustling St. John's Market (the pitch-roofed buildings on the left). The area was a network of busy streets filled with interesting buildings and small businesses.

Clayton Square

St. John's Market closed in 1964 to make way for a new shopping precinct. Based on the American shopping mall, the idea was to offer a wide range of shops under one roof. To create space for their new concept, the planners removed a whole area of history and character. Although the recent refurbishment has improved the look of the Precinct, it cannot compensate for what was one of the greatest attacks on the city's heritage.

Clayton Square, 1947

Littlewood's Cafe closed down, Brown's moved out and the News Theatre briefly became a Catholic church before the bulldozers moved in.

Clayton Square

The new Clayton Square Precinct has been well received. Its light and airy interior is complimented by an exterior that fits well into the Square. Pedestrianistion and the introduction of interesting paving and trees have helped to upgrade the overall setting.

Junction of Elliot Street and Lime Street, 1963

Another photograph of the market area before it was comprehensively redevloped.

Elliot Street

St. John's Precinct began trading in 1970. Ironically, St. John's Beacon, the concrete column towering above it, was opened to the public on April 1st 1971, a fitting day for such a folly.

St. George's Place, 1957

How many jobs did this short stretch of hotels, restaurants and shops support? A lively mix of interesting buildings and job-creating businesses is the formula that today's planners are trying to create in run-down central areas.

Roe Street

St. George's Place no longer exists. An ugly advertising hoarding and an even uglier car park are the 1970's contribution to the city's heritage.

Roe Street, 1962

The Royal Court was at the centre of market activity. The proliferation of small premises encouraged a network of business to start up and thrive.

Roe Street

The Royal Court has survived and still functions as a concert-hall, but the redevelopment swept away the smaller buildings around it.

Upper Dawson Street, 1961

The Theatre Royal opened in 1772 as the first provincial repertory theatre and the greatest performers of their time, including Charles Dickens and Paganini, trod its boards. Eventually, it fell out of use as a theatre and became a cold storage warehouse but even that was a less ignominious fate than that which finally befell it.

Dawson Street

Dawson Street is just the name given to a stretch of dual carriageway. Somewhere, under the tarmac, are the foundations of the Theatre Royal.

Lord Street, 1900

St. George's Church dominates the street scene. Built in 1774 and erected on the site of Liverpool Castle, it was substantially modified in 1821.

Lord Street

St. George's was pulled down in 1901 to make way for a very ordinary statue of Queen Victoria. Lord Street was badly damaged during the Blitz and virtually the whole eastern side was destroyed. The austere 1950's offices and shops reflect their time, although pedestrianisation has somewhat softened their look.

Corner of Whitechapel and Church Street, 1952

Bunney's could never be called an architectural masterpiece but it had a flamboyance and verve that makes the most of its prominent position.

Corner of Whitechapel and Church Street

Bunney's was demolished to make way for this inoffensive but bland exercise in modernism. New building in city centres is important but key sites like this deserve better.

Church Street, 1886

Church Street is named after St. Peter's Church (on the right) which was built in 1704 on open countryside. Compton Hotel, on the left, started its life as a department store before bankruptcy forced the owners to sell up.

Church Street

St. Peter's Church became the pro-cathedral of Liverpool until work commenced on the new building. Surplus to requirements and representing a valuable asset in the main shopping street, St. Peter's fell victim to new cathedral's need for building funds. In 1921, it was demolished to make way for a new Woolworth's store. Compton Hotel has reverted to its original use and is now a branch of Marks and Spencer.

Bold Street, c.1890

Bold Street is named after Tom Bold, a local Tory, and was originally used as a rope-walk. It was transformed into a shopping street in the early nineteenth century and became known as the 'Bond Street of the North'. The Lyceum, at the bottom of the street, was designed by Thomas Harrison of Chester and housed Liverpool Library, the first circulating library in Europe, and the Lyceum Gentlemen's Club. On the left, is the imposing entrance to Central Station.

Bold Street

Central Station facade was pulled down to make way for a very ordinary shopping block. Incredibly, it was proposed that the Lyceum should be demolished to add on further unwanted retail units. Only a spirited campaign and the late intervention of the Department of the Environment saved this important building. Bold Street is beginning to show signs of recovery and the recent decline appears to have been halted.